The Mother Kangaroo

by Edith Thacher Hurd

Illustrated by Clement Hurd

Boston Little, Brown and Company Toronto

Books in the Mother Animal Series

THE MOTHER BEAVER
THE MOTHER DEER
THE MOTHER WHALE
THE MOTHER OWL
THE MOTHER KANGAROO

ILLUSTRATIONS COPYRIGHT © 1976 BY CLEMENT HURD

TEXT COPYRIGHT © 1976 BY EDITH THACHER HURD

FIRST EDITION

T 08/76

Library of Congress Cataloging in Publication Data

Hurd, Edith Thacher.
  The mother kangaroo.

  (Mother animal series)
  SUMMARY: Describes the dependent relationship of a
joey to his mother until he grows old enough to leave
her and join a kangaroo mob of his own.
  1. Kangaroos — Behavior — Juvenile literature.
2. Parental behavior in animals — Juvenile literature.
[1. Kangaroos — Habits and behavior. 2. Parental
behavior in animals] I. Hurd, Clement, 1908–
II. Title.
QL737.M35H84   599'.2   75-44052
ISBN 0-316-38326-0

*Published simultaneously in Canada
by Little, Brown & Company (Canada) Limited*

PRINTED IN THE UNITED STATES OF AMERICA

The Mother Kangaroo

The sun shone hot in the big, wide sky.

The mother kangaroo lay in the shade of a small tree. She was resting and waiting.

Her young kangaroo, called a joey, sat close to her. He was eight months old and too big to live in her pouch anymore. But he still drank the special rich milk that would help him to grow into a strong kangaroo. He drank from a teat that he could reach from outside the pouch.

The mother kangaroo waited all day. While she
waited, she licked herself, cleaning her blue-
gray fur and the inside of her empty pouch.

The hot sun went down. The cool night came. The mother kangaroo stretched her long tail out in front of her and sat quietly, as her new baby was born.

The baby was tiny, not even one inch long. It did not have fur like its mother but was pink and soft all over. It had a big head and strong little front legs.

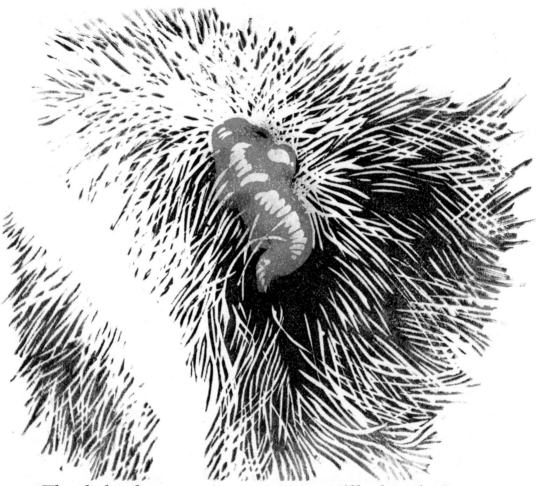

The baby kangaroo's eyes were still closed. It could not see where it was going. But it began to move as soon as it was born. It climbed with its sharp little claws, up, up through the long fur until it came to the soft darkness of its mother's pouch.

The baby took one of the four teats in its mouth and began to drink the special, thin, baby-kangaroo milk. It would keep this same teat in its mouth until it was six months old.

The mother kangaroo licked the tiny baby and cleaned herself all over. Then she began to hop slowly toward the billabong, or water hole, because she was thirsty. Her young joey hopped beside her.

The mother hopped on her hind legs with long jumps. But sometimes she stopped to walk slowly, putting her front feet on the ground so that she could graze on the fresh green grass.

When the mother kangaroo got to the billabong, she found a group, or "mob," of kangaroos already drinking. A big red male kangaroo and three females looked up at the mother kangaroo as she came close to the billabong.

Sometimes the mother kangaroo moved with this small mob. Sometimes she joined a very big mob of as many as one hundred kangaroos. It was safer for the mother kangaroo and her joey and baby to live with a mob.

The mother kangaroo crouched at the billabong, drinking. Suddenly, she heard the big red kangaroo make a coughing noise deep in his throat. The mother kangaroo knew that this was a warning of danger. She sat up and listened. Far, far away, she heard the barking of the fierce wild dogs, the dingoes. The dingoes were fast runners.

The red kangaroo turned from the billabong and started hopping with big leaps, going faster and faster. The mother kangaroo and the rest of the mob heard his hind feet thumping the ground. This was another warning that the dingoes were coming.

The mother kangaroo followed the red kangaroo, swinging her strong hind legs forward and back with high jumps over the ground. She ran until she could hardly run anymore.

At last the big red kangaroo stopped. He sat up
on his hind legs and tail. The mother kangaroo
stopped and looked for her joey. When she found
him, at the back of the mob, she sat quietly, lis-
tening for the dingoes. But she could not hear
them or see them. The mob had run too fast for
the wild dogs to catch them.

All this time, while the mother kangaroo was running so hard, the baby was safe in her pouch. The baby lay still and drank milk when it was hungry and each day it grew bigger. When it was two months old, its hind legs had grown longer and stronger than its little front legs. But it did not have any fur yet and its eyes were still closed.

Then, at last, when it was five months old, the baby began to sit up. It was covered all over with soft brown fur now and its eyes were wide open.

The baby poked its little head out of its mother's pouch and looked around at the world.

Not long after that, the baby gave a big push and
began hopping about, in little leaps and jumps,
close to its mother. Now the baby kangaroo be-
came the mother's new little joey. The older joey
had already grown up and gone off to find a mob
of his own.

The new little joey followed his mother when she was grazing and when she went to the billabong. But even though he was so young, he already knew about the danger signals. When he heard the deep cough of an old kangaroo or the pounding of his mother's feet on the hard ground, he hopped to her as fast as he could and disappeared into her pouch.

Sometimes the joeys played with each other. Standing on their hind legs and strong tails, they boxed with each other. Sometimes they hopped and leaped to see how high and how far they could go.

But one night the little joey hopped, and he
hopped, until at last he did not know where he
was. He could not find his mother. He made a
loud squeaking noise, calling for her to come
to him.

Three other kangaroos, who had heard him, came to find the little joey, but none of them was his mother.

The little joey sat very still. He did not know which way to go. He was very tired. He lay down on the grass but he could not go to sleep. He had never slept all alone outside of his mother's pouch before. High over his head, the bright stars shone in the dark sky.

At last, far away, he heard a thumping as if something were coming. Then he heard a soft clucking noise and he smelled the good smell that he knew was his mother. And then she was there, close beside him. The little joey gave a great hop and the mother kangaroo held her pouch open for him.

The joey lived with his mother until he was eight months old. After that he drank her milk but he did not go back into the pouch because the mother kangaroo had mated with the big red kangaroo and a new baby had been born. By the time he was one year old, the joey left his mother to find a mob of his own.

The baby grew until it was time for it to leave the pouch and to become the mother kangaroo's new joey, just as the one before, and the one before that had done.

And so the mother kangaroo lived under the big,
wide, Australian sky for the rest of her life. She
had many babies and each of these had many,
many babies and many joeys of their own.

HOW A KANGAROO GROWS

ONE MONTH   A baby kangaroo is born after it has been inside its mother for one month. It is only three-quarters of an inch long, about as big as a peanut.

FIVE MONTHS   The baby kangaroo pokes its head out of the mother's pouch for the first time.

SIX MONTHS   The baby kangaroo begins to leave the pouch for a little while every day.

EIGHT MONTHS   The baby kangaroo, now called a joey, leaves the pouch but still drinks milk.

ONE YEAR   The joey can now eat grass and does not need to drink milk. It begins to go off alone or with other joeys and soon leaves its mother.